Legends of the West: The Life and Legacy of Calamity Jane

By Charles River Editors

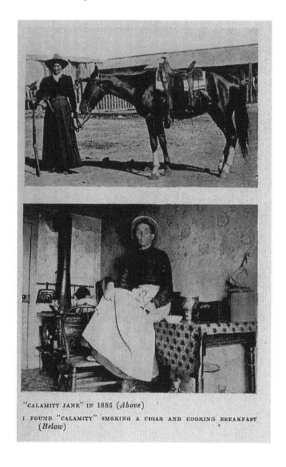

"CALAMITY JANE" IN 1885 (*Above*)
I FOUND "CALAMITY" SMOKING A CIGAR AND COOKING BREAKFAST (*Below*)

D1366998

About Charles River Editors

Charles River Editors was founded by Harvard and MIT alumni to provide superior editing and original writing services, with the expertise to create digital content for publishers across a vast range of subject matter. In addition to providing original digital content for third party publishers, Charles River Editors republishes civilization's greatest literary works, bringing them to a new generation via ebooks.

Introduction

Calamity Jane (circa 1852/6-1903)

"When fired upon Capt. Egan was shot. I was riding in advance and on hearing the firing turned in my saddle and saw the Captain reeling in his saddle as though about to fall. I turned my horse and galloped back with all haste to his side and got there in time to catch him as he was falling. I lifted him onto my horse in front of me and succeeded in getting him safely to the Fort. Capt Egan on recovering, laughingly said: 'I name you Calamity Jane, the heroine of the plains.' I have borne that name up to the present time." – Calamity Jane

Space may be the final frontier, but no frontier has ever captured the American imagination like the "Wild West", which still evokes images of dusty cowboys, outlaws, gunfights, gamblers, and barroom brawls over 100 years after the West was settled. A constant fixture in American pop culture, the 19th century American West continues to be vividly and colorful portrayed not just as a place but as a state of mind. In Charles River Editors' Legends of the West series, readers can get caught up to speed on the lives of America's most famous frontier figures in the time it takes to finish a commute, while learning interesting facts long forgotten or never known.

The most famous woman of the Wild West was also possibly the most colorful and mysterious. "Considered a remarkable good shot and a fearless rider for a girl of my age", Calamity Jane claimed to be a veteran of the Indian Wars, a scout, and the wife of Wild Bill Hickok, all on the way to becoming a dime novel heroine. While all of those legends have stuck, it's unclear to what extent if any they are actually true, and even her contemporaries doubted the authenticity of her statements. More than anything, people in frontier towns like Deadwood looked on with amusement at the girl who was more often than not drunk and was described by one of Wild Bill's friends as "simply a notorious character, dissolute and devilish." Her frequent drinking binges and her insistence that messing with her would "court calamity" had helped establish her nickname even before she arrived in Deadwood in the mid-1870s.

Ultimately, Calamity Jane's tall tales, eccentric personality, and association with Wild Bill would all make her a popular figure in the last quarter of the 19th century, and she became so well known that she started taking part in traveling shows of the kind made famous by Buffalo Bill Cody, where spectators could hear her colorfully (and drunkenly) talk about her life in the Wild West, with each telling stretching the truth ever further. Her legacy continued to crystallize after her death and eventually turn her into a legend, immortalized in countless dime novels, books, TV and the silver screen, helping make some of her contemporaries and surroundings notorious as well.

Legends of the West: The Life and Legacy of Calamity Jane chronicles the Western icon's life and examines the myths and legends in an attempt to separate fact from fiction. Along with pictures of important people, places, and events in his life, you will learn about Calamity Jane like you never have before, in no time at all.

Calamity Jane in 1895

Chapter 1: Calamity Jane's Early Years

The life of Martha Canary is so filled with uncertainties, myths, and misconceptions that even her given name, date of birth and place of birth are all up for debate. Martha herself seemed unclear on the details, but United States census reports indicate that Martha was born sometime in 1852 or 1856 in Princeton, Missouri. Her mother Charlotte was 16 years old when Martha was born, making her 19 years younger than Martha's father Robert. A younger brother, sister, and Martha's grandfather James also lived with the Canarys when Martha was a toddler. Like many families, the Canarys had made their way to Missouri from Ohio, possibly searching for cheaper land in the expanding western frontier.

Although the Canarys were not a permanent fixture in Princeton, they were memorable, but not in a good way. Even well into the 20th century, descendants of Bob and Charlotte avoided discussing Charlotte's behavior, which included smoking cigars, swearing, and drinking. If Bob Canary, a farmer by trade, was shocked at his young wife's behavior, he probably should not have been. Reports are that he met her at a saloon or perhaps a brothel and was so taken by her beauty that he thought he could reform her. For her own part, the autobiographical pamphlet attributed to Calamity said of her childhood, "As a child I always had a fondness for adventure and out-door exercise and especial fondness for horses which I began to ride at an early age and continued to do so until I became an expert rider being able to ride the most vicious and stubborn of horses, in fact the greater portion of my life in early times was spent in this manner."

Sometime between 1862 and 1864, the Canarys left Princeton, possibly due to a legal dispute involving Bob's unpaid debt. From there they may have moved on to Iowa, but in 1864 the gold rush called and the Canarys moved to the gold fields of Montana. How they afforded the move is unclear, because estimates are that for a family of four a move of this nature would have cost at least $600. That was a princely sum for the poor Canary family, but they told an army scout along the trail to Montana that they hoped to stake a claim and make their money there. Evidently, they never did strike it rich because on December 31, 1864, a Virginia City newspaper reported that three girls, most likely Martha and her two younger sisters, appeared on the doorstep of James Fergus. The man was known to be one of Madison County's commissioners responsible for administering to the poor.

Mrs. Fergus and two other women gave the poorly dressed girls food and clothing before sending them back to the mining camp where they lived. Meanwhile, the local paper described the parents as "inhuman brutes" that deserted their children, and the mother was singled out as "a woman of the lowest grade." Given the description of the mother, which matches up with what others said of Charlotte Canary, and the fact that the harsh winter sent the price of food rising in Montana that winter, it seems nearly certain that the family in question was indeed the Canarys.

Exactly what became of Martha's family is unknown. Her mother is believed to have contracted pneumonia and died in the mining camp settlement of Blackfoot City in the spring of 1866, but it is unclear where or when her father died, and it's unknown where her sisters ended up. It has long been assumed that they were adopted after they were left orphans due to the death of their parents, but there is no definite answer regarding what happened to them. Records support the notion that between 1864 and 1869, Martha spent most if not all of her time in Wyoming and Montana. It is possible that she briefly lived in Wyoming Territory with Major Patrick Gallagher and his wife, Frances, who reportedly picked up a girl along the trail in Fort Bridger in 1865. The Gallaghers were not able to control the girl they took in, which certainly fit the bill so far as Martha was concerned, and a group of miners collected enough cash to eventually send the girl to live among Union Pacific railroad workers.

This began a period of Martha's life that would repeat itself several times over. Despite tales that she as at various times a scout for the U.S. army, many of which were perpetuated by Martha herself, it's far more likely she was really just a so-called "camp follower." She followed the mining expeditions, railroad camps, and military posts of the West, often showing up right around payday. While some of the early accounts about Martha described her as "extremely attractive" and a "pretty, dark-eyed girl", *The Black Hills Daily Times* later described her far less glowingly as looking like the "result of a cross between the gable end of a fire proof and a Sioux Indian." Regardless of how attractive she could have been, it's apparent that Martha didn't mind exhibiting a masculine appearance and behavior, and she was most at home in the saloons where she could say, "Give me a shot of booze and slop it over the brim."[1]

This was also about the time that Martha Canary earned her famous nickname Calamity Jane and the reputation for wearing male clothing (although she actually wore dresses most of the time). She would later claim to have received the nickname during her service in the Indian Wars:

"It was on Goose Creek, Wyoming where the town of Sheridan is now located. Capt. Egan was in command of the Post. We were ordered out to quell an uprising of the Indians, and were out for several days, had numerous skirmishes during which six of the soldiers were killed and several severely wounded. When on returning to the Post we were ambushed about a mile and a half from our destination. When fired upon Capt. Egan was shot. I was riding in advance and on hearing the firing turned in my saddle and saw the Captain reeling in his saddle as though about to fall. I turned my horse and galloped back with all haste to his side and got there in time to catch him as he was falling. I lifted him onto my horse in front of me and succeeded in getting him safely to the Fort. Capt[.] Egan on recovering, laughingly said: 'I name you Calamity Jane, the heroine of the plains.' I have borne that name up to the present time."

Martha constantly claimed to have been a scout and a veteran of the Indian Wars, claiming, "I had a great many adventures with the Indians, for as a scout I had a great many dangerous missions to perform and while I was in many close places always succeeded in getting away safely for by this time I was considered the most reckless and daring rider and one of the best shots in the western country." However, Captain Jack Crawford, a friend of Wild Bill's and an actual Indian Wars veteran, told Montana's *Anaconda Standard* that Martha "never saw service in any capacity under either General Crook or General Miles. She never saw a lynching and never was in an Indian fight."

---

[1] *Deadwood Magazine*

Captain Jack

So how did Martha Canary become Calamity Jane? The answer is probably tawdry. At the time, men who solicited prostitutes were called Johns, and the prostitutes were called Janes, so far from being a unique nickname, Calamity Jane was a rather common one given to women known for their bawdy behavior. Martha earned money as an entertainer, a gambler, and a prostitute, or she relied on the generosity of friends and other people if she was really in need. Her fame came to her much the same way it did to other characters of the West; it was created by writers of the East who could not get enough of the tales from the western frontier. Whether the stories were true or not mattered little.

The first time Martha was referred to as Jane in print was in an article about the Black Hills Expedition in the *Chicago Tribune* in June 1875, when J.R. Lane called her "Jane Canary." Lane also mentioned that Martha was caring for one of her younger brothers, and he made mention of a demon that pursued Martha throughout her life: alcohol. While some of the details are wrong, the story of her dressed in a blue soldier's suit riding a mule is likely true. In fact, when her behavior got her into trouble, it was almost always because of her overindulgence in alcohol.

Chapter 2: Calamity Jane and Wild Bill Hickok

It's unclear whether Calamity Jane would have been famous without being associated with some of the company she kept, most notably James Butler "Wild Bill" Hickok. As with Calamity Jane, separating fact from fiction when it comes to the life of Wild Bill is nearly impossible, something due in great measure to the fact that the man himself exaggerated his own adventures or fabricated stories altogether.

Wild Bill Hickok

The best known aspects of Hickok's life hardly distinguish him from other famous Westerners. Like so many others, Hickok headed west as a fugitive of justice, yet that didn't prevent him from becoming a frontier lawman in Kansas, like Wyatt Earp. Hickok also became well known in the West for being a professional gambler and a remarkably quick draw who proved quite deadly in shootouts, like Doc Holliday.

What made Hickok stand out from so many of his day was that he was both successful at what he did and he managed to cultivate his own legend through tales of his exploits. By the mid-1870s, Hickok was notorious enough that he went out of his way to play cards with his back to the wall so he could see anyone approaching him. On one of the few occasions he did not, August 2, 1876, he was shot in the back of the head by Jack McCall while holding two pair, Aces and Eights (all black), now known as the Dead Man's Hand.

The relationship between Calamity Jane and Wild Bill has long been the stuff of legends, and much of it is the result of total embellishment. What is true is that the stories about Calamity Jane and Wild Bill Hickok resulted from the chase for gold in the Black Hills of South Dakota.

Deadwood, in the Black Hills of South Dakota, was like many mining towns, save for the fact that it was not supposed to be there. In 1874, General George Armstrong Custer led a troop over of 1,000 men to investigate reports of the discovery of gold on Lakota-Sioux land in the Black Hills. Sioux ownership of the land stemmed from the Treaty of Laramie in 1868, but the discovery of gold changed things for the United States. The mining town of Deadwood quickly sprung up as prospectors descended on the area, even though the federal government had ordered military troops to set up posts there to keep prospectors out.

Deadwood fell in the middle of a legal loophole because the boomtown was outside of U.S. jurisdiction. Maintaining law and order in Deadwood was a challenge because Deadwood was not even supposed to exist. Further complicating matters was the issue that Deadwood was on

Indian land. U.S. laws could not be passed, let alone enforced, on land that the U.S. did not possess. This made for a chaotic environment that relied on sporadic self-policing to try and keep some semblance of order, often with minimal success.

Though he was one of the most legendary gunmen of the West, Wild Bill was on the verge of blindness due to trachoma in 1876, and his gunfighting days were over by the time he first met Calamity Jane that year. Jane was still a camp follower in February 1876 when she became part of an expedition against the Lakota-Sioux that was led by General George Crook in Laramie, Wyoming. While other stories about her scouting have been disputed, it is known that during this one Jane swam the Platte River and rode hard 90 miles to deliver dispatches, working at such a frenzied pace that she eventually fell ill and had to spend weeks recuperating. Her autobiographical statement also claimed, "During the month of June I acted as a pony express rider carrying the U.S. mail between Deadwood and Custer, a distance of fifty miles, over one of the roughest trails in the Black Hills country. As many of the riders before me had been held up and robbed of their packages, mail and money that they carried, for that was the only means of getting mail and money between these points. It was considered the most dangerous route in the Hills, but as my reputation as a rider and quick shot was well known, I was molested very little, for the toll gatherers looked on me as being a good fellow, and they knew that I never missed my mark. I made the round trip every two days which was considered pretty good riding in that country."

Hickok, meanwhile, had recently married the former circus performer Agnes Lake, but he left his new bride in Cincinnati while he took a train back to Laramie in late spring in 1876. His plan was to join the gold rush headed for the Black Hills, and in June he got ready to leave Laramie to join his friend, Charlie Utter, on a wagon train that was leaving for South Dakota.

At the time, getting to the Black Hills was not easy. Bugs referred to as "sand gnats" continually buzzed around travelers, not to mention the problems that the deep gulches along the trail and the cold drizzling rain caused. The trip presented additional challenges because just as Utter and Hickok reached Fort Laramie, news came down from the Black Hills that Custer had been killed in Montana at the Battle of Little Big Horn. Indian attacks were not uncommon as the Lakota-Sioux attempted to protect their land from invasion by prospectors.

Due to the heightened awareness of trouble with Indians, the military suggested to Utter and Hickok that they join a larger group also going toward the Black Hills, which would provide them some additional protection against a possible attack. An officer also asked Hickok and Utter if they would take the wild woman that they had in the post guardhouse. As was typical for 20 year-old Jane, she had shown up at the fort right around payday and went on a drinking binge with some of the soldiers. As Hickok and Utter were discussing their plans to join the 30-wagon group looking for gold, she was sleeping off the effects of the alcohol, still partly drunk and partially naked. For whatever reason, the group agreed to take Jane along. The army provided her with military underwear and the wagon train, with no other clothing available for a woman, gave her a buckskin suit. Photographs of her in this suit perpetuated the idea that Martha dressed in men's clothing, although in this instance it was because she had no other choice.

Calamity Jane in her buckskin

Jane was not the only camp follower with the group. In fact, she was one of about a dozen women who were for all intents and purposes ladies of the evening, including well-known ladies like Madam Moustache and Dirty Em. Jane was mostly the primary companion to Steve Utter on the two-week trip, and occasionally she was with Charlie Utter, but by all accounts there was no romance of any type between her and Wild Bill. This was the first time he had ever seen her, and for the most part he merely tolerated her presence, although he appreciated that she helped out the wagon train by cooking meals. She proved to be a valuable mule-team driver, helping get the team over some rough spots, and she was indeed a good shot too. In the evening, when the men gathered around the fire to drink and tell stories, she was at home in that environment just as much as they were.

Many of the men found her tales, which were spiced up with cuss words not typically heard coming from a lady's mouth, quite entertaining. But Hickok was not one of those men. He was quiet most of the trip and had little to do with Martha, other than when she came around to get her tin cup filled from the keg of whiskey that he bought for the trip. When she needed a refill, she needed to see him, and at one point he told her to slow down and save some for the rest of the men. When the group reached Custer City, the southern region of the Black Hills, the few residents that had remained after finding out about the gold in nearby Deadwood thought little of Hickok. A newspaper reported that he looked like a bum, and the women he was with, including Jane, were not much better.

The group arrived in Deadwood around July 12 and made quite a spectacle of their arrival as they paraded down Main Street dressed in buckskin suits. But it was the arrival of Calamity Jane that a July 15 edition of the *Black Hills Pioneer* was most excited to report, with a headline blaring, "Calamity Jane has arrived!". No other members of her traveling party were mentioned by name at all, although this was not her first trip to Deadwood either. In 1875 she had accompanied the Walter Jenney expedition there, apparently snuck into the group by one of the soldiers. Few women could be found in mining towns, so when a woman arrived in a town like Deadwood it was news, especially a woman like Calamity Jane.

Now that she was there, she immediately became a popular dance hall girl, despite her rather masculine appearance. She became part of the hurdy-gurdy houses, where young ladies served as dance partners for the male patrons. There was no charge for the dancing, but following the dance it was expected that the men take their dance partners to the bar to buy drinks. The ladies and the proprietor of the dance house shared in the profits from the drinks. One prospector recalled seeing Jane wearing a fancy Stetson hat and a purple handkerchief as she danced with nearly everyone in the saloon, and then proceeded to the bar after every dance. It was also not an uncommon sight for Jane to dance with the women, just as the men did.

While it was not an automatic assumption that the dance hall girls were also prostitutes, it was not unheard of for some of the women to make extra money this way. One notorious proprietor, Al Swearingen, opened the "Gem Theater", a dance hall, in May 1876, and Jane was one of only three available dancers. In fact, the available pool of women for the dance hall was so slim that a young man dressed as a woman served as a dancer for a while. A bartender named Sam Young said that Jane once agreed to go to Sidney, Nebraska to round up more women for the Gem.

After exaggerating the details about the money that could be made in Deadwood, Jane returned to town with ten young girls ready to work for Swearengen.

The Gem Theater circa 1876

Jane did not camp out on the edge of town with Hickok and his fellow prospectors when they arrived in the summer of 1876, but she did return often for food, and the men later loaned her money so she could buy something to wear other than her buckskin suit. She pleaded her case, saying that she could hardly compete with the other women if she was not dressed properly, so Wild Bill kicked in $20 with the special request that she "wash behind her ears." After she earned some money from her exploits in the saloons and dance halls, she returned to the camp, wearing a dress and stockings, from which she produced a roll of cash. She said business had been good and paid some of the men back, although Hickok refused to take any of the money, remarking, "At least she looks like a woman now."[2]

Much of Calamity Jane's reputation ultimately came from her time in Deadwood. In one

---

[2] McLaird, James D. *Calamity Jane: The Woman and the Legend.* Page 59.

memorable scene, another member of Wild Bill's party, a woman named "Tid Bit," had agreed to spend time with a man called Laughing Sam. He paid her in gold dust, which ended up being a combination of sand and brass filings. Upon hearing of this, Jane borrowed Charley's two ivory-handled six-shooters and went to the saloon where she knew she would find Laughing Sam running a game of faro. Guns in hand, Jane burst into the saloon and proceeded to cuss out Laughing Sam until he agreed to give Tid Bit two twenty-dollar gold pieces.

Meanwhile, few if any members of Hickok's group recalled him actually prospecting for gold. He did some target shooting in the woods in the morning and still had enough skill to impress a reporter with his ability to shoot a tomato can out of the air. The reporter, Leander Richardson from *The Springfield Republican* in Massachusetts, confirmed that Calamity Jane was enamored with Charlie Utter, called Colorado Charlie, not Hickok. Like Hickok, Charlie was a snappy dresser, had long blonde hair, and fascinated the locals with his morning ritual of taking a bath, a completely unique habit back then. Utter was also as neat with his surroundings as he was with his appearance and kept a very tidy tent. One night after a drunken binge, Hickok went into Charlie's tent and fell asleep on his bed, which was made with fine linens and a blanket. When Charlie found him, he dragged Hickok out by his feet and deposited him on the ground.

At this point in his life, Hickok was most likely an alcoholic. Before he could begin his day, he needed a drink and could be seen with his hair tied back into a knot, gun shoved into his belt, running toward the saloon to get a stash of liquor to bring back to his tent to help him get dressed and complete his morning routine. He was also addicted to poker, but some suggested that he was out of his league with the professional players in Deadwood.

Fittingly, the death of Wild Bill Hickok is shrouded in legend and mystery, and it's still not completely clear why he was shot by Broken Nose Jack McCall. It is believed that in a poker game on or around August 1, 1876, Hickok took all of the 24 year-old McCall's money. Allegedly, Hickok gave McCall a bit of his money back so that he could eat, but not before scolding McCall for betting more money than he had to lose. This was said to have enraged the young man.

Hickok was in Deadwood on August 2, 1876 to take part in a friendly card game at Saloon No. 10. To show how far Hickok's stock had fallen by the time he got to Deadwood, he found himself sitting with his back to the door, a table position he would never allow himself to take in the old days. Wild Bill had a habit of sitting with his back to a wall so he could see anyone and everyone coming toward him, a habit he had developed when he was making enemies as a marshal. This time, Wild Bill twice asked Charles Rich to change chairs with him, but he was ignored. A decade earlier, Hickok would only have had to direct a man to move, and he would have done so out of fear and/or respect.

The location of Saloon No. 10

It's possible that Hickok wouldn't have stood a chance even with his back to the wall. As the game progressed, nobody paid any attention to Jack McCall, an indication that nobody had any reason to suspect he had a score to settle. As the table was playing 5 card draw, McCall approached Hickok from behind, shouted "Take that!" and fired a shot into the back of Hickok's head, killing him instantly. The shot was from such close range that the bullet exited Hickok's cheek and struck one of the other players, Captain Massie, in the wrist. As Hickok's lifeless body slumped onto the table, his cards fell from his hand, revealing two pair, black Aces and black 8s. Though a full house of Jacks over 10s used to be known back then as the Dead Man's Hand, Hickok's legendary death and hand eclipsed it, and Aces and 8s have been known as Dead

Man's Hand since Wild Bill's legend took off. Charlie Utter would claim the body and file a notice in the *Black Hills Pioneer*, "Died in Deadwood, Black Hills, August 2, 1876, from the effects of a pistol shot, J. B. Hickock (Wild Bill) formerly of Cheyenne, Wyoming. Funeral services will be held at Charlie Utter's Camp, on Thursday afternoon, August 3, 1876, at 3 o'clock P. M. All are respectfully invited to attend."

In the aftermath of Wild Bill's death, Jane made one of her wilder claims:

My friend, Wild Bill, remained in Deadwood during the summer with the exception of occasional visits to the camps. On the 2nd of August, while setting at a gambling table in the Bell Union saloon, in Deadwood, he was shot in the back of the head by the notorious Jack McCall, a desperado. I was in Deadwood at the time and on hearing of the killing made my way at once to the scene of the shooting and found that my friend had been killed by McCall. I at once started to look for the assassin and found him at Shurdy's butcher shop and grabbed a meat cleaver and made him throw up his hands; through the excitement on hearing of Bill's death, having left my weapons on the post of my bed. He was then taken to a log cabin and locked up, well secured as every one thought, but he got away and was afterwards caught at Fagan's ranch on Horse Creek, on the old Cheyenne road and was then taken to Yankton, Dak., where he was tried, sentenced and hung.

In reality, Jane had nothing to do with catching McCall. After stunningly shooting Hickok, McCall backed out of the saloon with his gun raised and made his way to his horse, but the cinch was loose and McCall fell to the ground. He ran for cover in the butcher shop but was discovered by a group of locals. McCall claimed that he shot Hickok in revenge for the death of his own brother in Kansas, but there is no evidence that he had a brother. Some say his feelings were bruised over the remarks Hickok made to him about betting over his head. Whatever the reason, an impromptu trial was held the next day among the local miners in the town. Even though there was no official law enforcement in Deadwood, the citizens tried to maintain some form of order with familiar mechanisms, such as jury trials. Despite overwhelming evidence that McCall killed Hickok in cold blood, he pleaded his case, saying that he was exacting revenge for his brother's death and that Hickok claimed that he would kill him too. Incredibly, McCall was declared innocent and set free, and he promptly left town, no doubt wary of retribution from Hickok's friends. In response to the verdict, the *Black Hills Pioneer* editorialized, "Should it ever be our misfortune to kill a man ... we would simply ask that our trial may take place in some of the mining camps of these hills."

The day after the trial, Charlie Utter arranged for Hickok's funeral. Wild Bill was laid out in a beautiful coffin in a tee-pee, where his friends and the people of Deadwood congregated to pay their last respects to one of the West's most famous icons. The grave marker read, "Wild Bill, J.

B. Hickock killed by the assassin Jack McCall in Deadwood, Black Hills, August 2, 1876. Pard, we will meet again in the happy hunting ground to part no more. Good bye, Colorado Charlie, C. H. Utter."

Steve and Charlie Utter at Wild Bill's grave

McCall refused to simply consider himself lucky to get away with murder. When he made it to Wyoming, he continued to talk about his one claim to fame and bragged about the killing of Wild Bill Hickok. When officials in Wyoming heard about it, they did not accept the verdict from the citizen court in Deadwood. McCall was formally charged and extradited to Yankton, South Dakota. Since Deadwood was not a legal jurisdiction, it was claimed that trying him would not be double jeopardy. Thus McCall stood trial again, and this time he was found guilty. "The coward McCall hanged for the murder of Hickok on March 1, 1877. A reporter in town who claimed to talk to McCall filed a report (almost certainly wrongly) claiming, "As I write the closing lines of this brief sketch, word reaches me that the slayer of Wild Bill has been rearrested by the United State authorities, and after trial has been sentenced to death for willful murder. He is now at Yankton, D.T. awaiting execution. At the trial it was proved that the murderer was hired to do his work by gamblers who feared the time when better citizens should appoint Bill the champion of law and order – a post which he formerly sustained in Kansas border life, with credit to his manhood and his courage."

By 1902, Martha's exaggeration about her involvement with Hickok had progressed to marriage. Certainly her uncontrollable grief after Hickok's death, while sincere, contributed to the belief that Martha and Hickok had an intimate relationship, if not a marriage. Some say that she granted Hickok a divorce so he could marry Agnes Lake. However, in a 1902 interview she said that Hickok was her fiancé and that they were due to be married days after he was shot.

Claiming that law enforcement was doing nothing to locate Hickok's killer, she said she went to Yankton to bring the case against McCall to the grand jury and see that he was extradited and hanged for the murder. In reality, she was never married to Hickok, nor did she have anything to do with McCall's extradition to South Dakota.

Nevertheless, legend had it that when she died, her last words were to request that she be buried next to her husband Wild Bill, and people continued to run with it. In 1941, rumors of a relationship between Hickok and Calamity Jane persisted with the appearance of a woman saying that she was Jean Hickok McCormick. On May 6, McCormick went on the nationally broadcast CBS radio show "We the People" and said that she was the daughter of Wild Bill Hickok and Calamity Jane. She said she could prove it with a diary and letters written by Calamity Jane herself. Supposedly, this marriage occurred in Kansas in 1871 after Martha warned Hickok about a band of desperadoes headed his way, and then tended to his wounds after the battle. The documents claimed that a Reverend Warren married Martha and Hickok on the Kansas prairie, witnessed by several other men. The good reverend reportedly used a page from his Bible to scrawl out a marriage certificate. CBS Radio believed her and invited her to do a nationally broadcast interview. Apparently, the Billings Office of Public Welfare believed her, too, and gave her the old age assistance that she requested.

McCormick went on to say that Hickok did not want his marriage to Calamity Jane to become public knowledge because he did not want either his wife or daughter to be in harm's way and used against him by outlaws. Therefore, he kept both his marriage and the birth of his daughter, which McCormick said occurred in a secluded cabin in Montana, a secret. Hickok was somehow able to hire an Indian to find the cabin and help Martha tend to her newborn child. The family never lived together and according to McCormick, it was when Hickok and Martha reunited in Deadwood that she granted Hickok his divorce so that he could marry Agnes Lake.

As for McCormick, she said that her mother gave her up for adoption and went to live with James O'Neill, a Liverpool sea captain for the Cunard Line who was living in Richmond, Virginia. McCormick claims that Jane visited her twice, although she never revealed her true identity. The second of these meetings allegedly occurred when Calamity Jane was traveling with Buffalo Bill Cody's Wild West Show in Richmond. McCormick said that after that show, she traveled with her mother when the tour moved on to England. McCormick's story was enough to convince the Billings, Montana public welfare office, which granted her request for old age assistance.

McCormick may have shared Calamity Jane's propensity for tall stories, but she didn't inherit it. Calamity Jane and Wild Bill were never married, and they never had a daughter. Put simply, none of McCormick's story was true. It was a well-established fact in the 19th century that Jane was illiterate and thus would have been incapable of writing the letters and the diary that

McCormick produced, which were filled with flowing prose and proper grammar. There was no such person as Captain James O'Neill, and Calamity Jane, while she did know Bill Cody, was never part of his show. McCormick omits from her story that Calamity Jane was a known alcoholic, later married a man named Bill Steers and had a daughter named Jessie. Despite this, McCormick was buried in a Billings grave with a tombstone reading that she was the daughter of Wild Bill Hickok and Calamity Jane. Unfortunately, many people believed the fraudulent story, which continues to complicate the truth about Calamity Jane.

Chapter 3: Calamity Jane Finds Fame

While Jane made up quite a bit when it came to her time in Deadwood, one of her boasts was authentic, and it did rightly cast her in a heroic light:

"I remained around Deadwood locating claims, going from camp to camp until the spring of 1877, where one morning, I saddled my horse and rode towards Crook city. I had gone about twelve miles from Deadwood, at the mouth of Whitewood creek, when I met the overland mail running from Cheyenne to Deadwood. The horses on a run, about two hundred yards from the station; upon looking closely I saw they were pursued by Indians. The horses ran to the barn as was their custom. As the horses stopped I rode along side of the coach and found the driver John Slaughter, lying face downwards in the boot of the stage, he having been shot by the Indians. When the stage got to the station the Indians hid in the bushes. I immediately removed all baggage from the coach except the mail. I then took the driver's seat and with all haste drove to Deadwood, carrying the six passengers and the dead driver."

While Calamity Jane was notorious among her Western contemporaries, she actually became famous before the end of the 1870s thanks to the production of dime store novels, and it's not even clear what Calamity Jane was doing before her newly found fame. Reports are that she got married in Custer City, although it is not known who she was married to or how long she was in Custer City. Much of her fame can be attributed to the emergence of Calamity Jane as a dime novel character. Sold for between five and ten cents, dime novels were the precursor to pulp fiction, regaling readers with tall tales of the West. Most of the West's icons were portrayed in dime novels of the era, from lawmen like Wyatt Earp to outlaws like Billy the Kid, feeding into the country's desire for stories about the expanding frontier. Truth was not required.

In October 1877, Calamity Jane got her turn as a heroine in the popular Deadwood Dick series, published by Beadle and Adams. Over 1,100 of the soap opera-like tales from the West were published, and in the summer of 1877 the publishing house started a series that took place in the Black Hills. Edward Wheeler's Deadwood Dick series was one of the most popular runs, and Calamity Jane appeared alongside the title character. Wheeler wrote about 100 of the novels, and of the 33 Deadwood Dick books, Calamity Jane appeared in about half. She was presented as a woman of independent means and thinking, but her heart always belonged to Dick, and no matter what scrapes they got into, the plots always had a happy ending. Like modern-day soap operas, the dime novels were written sequentially, each one building on the plot of the previous book. Deadwood Dick marries four times in the series, and his fourth wife is Calamity Jane.

After the first book in the series was published, Calamity Jane became an instant celebrity, and everyone wanted a glimpse of one of the West's most wild women. Reporters began to request interviews, hoping to write articles that would sell their papers, but they were often surprised at the difference between the real Calamity Jane and the character of Calamity Jane. The Black Hills capitalized on Calamity Jane's fame too; Horatio N. Maguire, a local journalist, wrote a promotional pamphlet for the Black Hills that included an article on the colorful Calamity Jane, a woman he claimed to personally know. Maguire said that upon arriving for the first time in the Black Hills, he asked an old-timer how far it was to Deadwood. Maguire wrote that he was told to follow the girl on her horse that was up ahead, but all he saw was a "dare-devil boy." The old-timer said, "Why, that's a girl on that bucking cayuse; that's 'Calamity Jane.'" Maguire went on to embellish – if not outright invent – the description of Jane that day, saying, "There was nothing in her attire to distinguish her sex, as she sat astride the fiery horse she was managing with a cruel Spanish bit in his mouth, save her small neat-fitting gaiters, and sweeping raven locks."[3] The Deadwood Dick series drew heavily from Maguire's description of Calamity Jane.

Despite the fact that it was fiction, Maguire's description was also widely circulated in newspapers, including the *Rocky Mountain News* in Denver and the *Cheyenne Daily Leader.* Jane's reputation grew as articles about her spread, but there was also a growing faction of journalists that believed her reputation was based on lies. Dan Scott, who wrote for the *Daily Champion* in Deadwood, went so far as to call her a fraud and said "a hundred waiter girls and mop squeezers in this gulch are her superiors in anything the reader can name," adding "her form and features" were "not only indifferent but repulsive."[4] Scott admonished other newspapers for continuing to give her publicity that he believed was entirely unwarranted.

Scott's article did not go unnoticed by Jane, and thus began her battles with the press. The *Champion* was owned by Charley Collins, and after Scott's article was published, Jane allegedly went to the newspaper office and yelled at Scott so ferociously that he was afraid she might hit him. A few weeks later, she returned and took the photo of Collins from the wall, saying she was going to take it to one of the local saloons and have some fun with it. Collins went looking for her after he found out, but he could not get her to return the photo and he supposedly had to hide out for several days to escape her wrath. Like so many other stories about Jane, it is unclear if this an accurate story.

Still, not everyone found Jane to be so distasteful. Colonel Clement A. Lounsberry, a writer for the *Bismarck Tribune,* visited the Black Hills in August 1877 to do a story on the gold rush. Upon his visit to a local hurdy-gurdy house, he met Jane and not only danced with her but spoke with her at length. He did not find her to be as unattractive as Scott reported, and he pointed out the fact that she was an orphan who had grown up with adult supervision necessary to learn appropriate social skills. Lounsberry said that Jane told him that she had been married, but a fire destroyed their cabin and all of her belongings so she was forced back into her old way of life. Lounsberry concluded that she deserved kindness, not criticism. As the glowing portrayal suggests, Lounsberry also apparently spent some time courting Jane.

Chapter 4: Marriages

During the first three years after dime novels made her famous, Calamity Jane lived in the Dakota Territory in the Black Hills and at Fort Pierre. She had no permanent home and simply seemed to go where the action was, though due to her fame most local newspapers made mention of her whenever she was in town. One of the reports mistakenly announced her death in Denver after being thrown from a buggy, but the paper had the wrong Calamity Jane. As if her tall tales and colorful fabrications didn't make her life story harder to figure out, the fact that she was not the only woman known as Calamity Jane also tended to muddle the facts about her life.

---

[3] *Calamity Jane: The Woman and the Legend,* Page 88.
[4] *Calamity Jane: The Woman and the Legend,* Page 89.

On December 17, 1877, Martha Canary announced to a reporter from the *Black Hills Daily Times* that she was not Calamity Jane and now wanted to be known as Maggie Cosgrove because she had married George Cosgrove, a member of the wagon train led by Wild Bill Hickok and Steve Utter the year before. A local resident recalled that Martha and George spent the winter of 1876-1877 together in Sherman, Wyoming and that Martha said she married George in Cheyenne. Cosgrove was a native of Toronto, Canada and went to the U.S. with his parents when he was five years old. The Cosgroves migrated from Michigan to Wyoming, and then to the Black Hills with the wagon train. They prospected for a while and then hauled supplies along the Pierre-Deadwood Trail.

Martha reportedly was with George at a bar at a Hat Creek ranch when she yelled to the crowd that she was a married woman and was living a "straight" life now. But life as Mrs. Cosgrove apparently did not last long, because by January 1878 she reported that she was fed up with Deadwood and went to Rapid City, South Dakota to prospect for gold. However, by January 22 she was back in Deadwood and made her first visit to a photographic studio for a posed portrait. The next month she said she had left George Cosgrove for a man named Jim. Exactly who Jim was is not known, and Jim was not the only man to be with her during this time. Reports also claimed that she married Frank Lacy and lived with him for a time in Fort Fetterman, Wyoming, west of the Black Hills. Lacy had a government contract to haul wood to Fetterman, which was a lodging and supply facility for travelers.

Her fame continued to grow that same year when journalist Thomas Newson wrote "Drama of Life in the Black Hills," a one-act play with Calamity Jane as a central character. Newson included a biography of the 22 year-old woman, and unlike many writers of the era, he got the details about her correct. He wrote, in part, "She imitates no one; is an original in herself; despises hypocrisy; and is easily melted to tears. She is generous, forgiving, kind-hearted, sociable, and yet when aroused, has all the daring and courage of the lion or the devil himself…"[5] Not everything was accurate, though, as Newson perpetuated the notion that she served as a scout and fought the Indians.

Jane's most enduring, albeit stormy, relationship was with Bill Steers. Steers was born in Honey Creek, Iowa in 1865, making him at least nine years younger than her. As bad as her reputation was for causing trouble, Steers was at the very least her equal, and on more than one occasion Jane had him jailed for abuse. In Meeker, Colorado Steers stood trial for Jane's claims that he hit her with a rock and tried to stab her, to which he replied she was a liar and then proceeded to shred his coat. The judge fined Steers and sentenced him to a night in jail, a night Jane spent by getting drunk. Steers briefly left town, but he returned soon after that, and the next week people watched Steers and Jane set out together for Rawlins, Wyoming, with the young

[5] *Calamity Jane: The Woman and the Legend,* Page 103.

girl carrying their pack. The local paper was not pleased to see Steers after the events in Meeker and suggested that Jane was not as bad as advertised.

Six weeks later, Steers reportedly struck Jane again while the two were engaged in a drunken brawl, this time with a monkey wrench that left a serious gash on her head. When Martha swore out a complaint with local law enforcement, Steers headed toward Colorado and Jane headed toward the saloon, where she was escorted out after too many whiskeys. But she did not go quietly, throwing rocks through the plate glass window as she went. Steers was eventually tracked down and sentenced to 30 days in jail. The local paper opined that Steers got what he deserved, while lamenting that the law did not permit him to stay in jail even longer.

Calamity Jane continued to build upon her legend as a drinker. In a saloon in Rawlins, whiskey was called "Calamity water", and newspapers reported on her drinking exploits. In Cheyenne, she avoided a jail sentence by presenting the judge with a certificate confirming that she was pregnant, and it is assumed that the father of the child was Steers. In her autobiography, Jane said that her daughter Jessie was born on October 28, 1887 in or near Lander, Wyoming. The following spring, she had Steers jailed again for abuse in Green River, Wyoming, although she was also arrested for drunk and disorderly conduct. Where Jessie was while her parents got drunk and carried on in saloons is not clear; most likely she was left with friends or Steers' family.

At this point in time, Jane's relationship with Steers became muddled in history. It is known that Martha Canary and William Steers got married in Pocatello, Idaho on May 30, 1888, but after that there is no other mention of Steers being with her. In her autobiography, Jane said that she married a man named Clinton Burke in 1885 and that he, not Steers, was the father of Jessie. And for at least a while, Jessie lived with her mother in Deadwood; Jane had returned to Deadwood after a 16-year absence to try and get a spot in the Diamond Dick and Company Wild West Show, but she was not accepted. Contrary to widespread belief, Calamity Jane was never a performer in any of Buffalo Bill Cody's Wild West Shows either. Cody's shows provided credible talent to paying customers around the world, and Calamity Jane had no marketable skill that would have fit in his lineup. While she was acknowledged as a good shot, she wasn't a crack shot or a sharpshooter in the same vein as famous performers like Annie Oakley.

As for Jessie, Mrs. Osborne Pemberton went to school with her at St. Edward's Academy when they were children and recalled years later that the other children teased Jessie because of her mother. One day, as children were leaving church, Pemberton remembered that they chased Jessie and threw rocks at her while chanting "Calamity Jane, Calamity Jane." After just a few weeks, Jessie withdrew from school.

Exactly what happened to Jessie was not clear until Jessie Oakes from Los Angeles, California wrote to local historical societies asking for help in locating information about Calamity Jane, claiming that Calamity Jane was her grandmother. In fact, Calamity Jane was her mother. When Jessie was with her in Deadwood from 1895–1896 and Billings, Montana in the late 1890s, Jane may have intentionally told Jessie that she was her grandmother to spare her further teasing. Either Jane or Jessie created a story about Jessie's parents, because Jessie claimed that her mother was a beautiful woman who was a skilled shooter and rider, while her father was a handsome lieutenant in the U.S. Army. Jessie also said that she had a half-brother named Charles Jackson Oakes, but that they had been separated since they were small children. In addition to the fact that Jessie's description of a beautiful woman hardly fit Jane, there is no evidence to suggest Jane had a son. There were rumors that Jane had given birth to a son who died in infancy, but there is no evidence to support even that.

Chapter 5: Calamity Jane's Final Years

Even though Calamity Jane was not part of Buffalo Bill's Wild West Shows, she did manage to find ways to capitalize on her fame and draw an income. She contracted with the Kohl & Middleton Dime Museum Company out of Cincinnati to tour the country as part of the growing dime museum phenomenon. Not a traditional museum, dime museums featured live entertainment with up to five shows a day. Jane apparently contacted Charles Kohl and George Middleton to request a contract, and in 1896 they agreed to not only give her a contract but also a salary to her husband Clinton Burke. Burke was scheduled to accompany Jane, who was now also going by the name Martha Burke, while she made arrangements for Jessie to attend school in Sturgis when they were on tour.

Deadwood newspapers wished her well on her opening night at the Palace Museum in Minneapolis, but they expressed concern about her drinking given her frequent appearances in the saloons. Still, she completed her contractual agreement, and the handbills for the show showed her dressed in buckskin with a knife clenched between her teeth. The captions screamed out "The Famous Woman Scout of the West!", "Terror of Evildoers in the Black Hills!", and "The Comrade of Buffalo Bill and Wild Bill!" Of course, none of this was true, but that didn't stop her from giving a stage performance that consisted of her dressing up in buckskins and telling all the tales of her adventures that people wanted to hear. Naturally, with the passage of time and the consumption of alcohol, Jane's stories got progressively more fanciful.

Martha also sold her short autobiography "Life and Adventures of Calamity Jane," which was likely published that same year. It is not clear who helped Martha write the book, which is full of inaccuracies, fibs, and outright lies about her life. And while it is surprisingly accurate about true events that happened to occur when she was nearby, the problem was that she had little to do with those events other than be there. Nevertheless, her fans paid their few cents for the book and took it all as fact, as did many historians until more detailed research was done. Martha also discovered that pamphlets, photographs, and booklets about her sold well enough to help her make some cash.

Despite the fame and money, or perhaps because of it, by 1901 the woman known as Calamity Jane was a broken down alcoholic with no permanent home. A Bozeman, Montana newspaper had reported around this time that Mrs. Robert Dorsett had taken ill on a train and had to be taken to the county physician for an examination because she did not have any money to see a doctor. Robert Dorsett was another man that was supposedly a husband to Calamity Jane, although it may have been a common-law marriage. Still, the Calamity Jane name carried weight. Buffalo, New York, then the eighth-largest city in the U.S., was the site of the 1901 Pan-American Exposition from May-November of that year, and part of the fair's attractions was a midway featuring a variety of entertainers. The publicity department decided that it wanted Calamity Jane on its midway and hired a reporter named Josephine Brake to track her down and talk her into going to Buffalo.

Brake heard that Jane could be found at a poorhouse in Livingston, Montana, and everything she knew about the Western legend came from the embellished reports of her frontier adventures. Brake arrived first in Butte, and then in Livingston in July, shortly after Jane's Independence Day drinking binge. Newspaper accounts disagree on how Jane received her offer. The *Livingston Post* said that when Brake met Jane, she promised to set her up in an easy, luxurious life to allow her to "retire" in comfort. Jane didn't believe Brake at first, but after she was convinced that the offer to go east was real, she agreed and said she would "be a good girl all the rest of her life."[6]

Conversely, the *Butte Miner* said that it took considerable convincing to get Martha to leave the life she had grown accustomed to, regardless of how poor it was. The *Billings Times* also doubted the sincerity of Brake's intentions and was suspicious that Jane was simply being used for the publicity. The article said of Brake, "She has some scheme afoot and Calamity will bitterly regret leaving Montana. She will earn what she gets, but only for the woman who took her away. Some of the old pioneers ought to try and keep watch as to just where Calamity is taken."[7]

The concerns for her were valid. Troubles between Brake and Jane began before they reached Buffalo once Brake found out that the real Calamity Jane was a difficult woman to handle, especially when in need of a drink. Jane's wariness of the press did not help, either. But once she got there, Calamity Jane was a popular attraction in Buffalo, appearing in two parades along the midway and appearing as part of the expo's Indian Congress. The Congress featured expert sharp shooting, Indian races, and mock battles, which regularly filled its 25,000-seat arena. Even though she was part of the show, Calamity Jane was not mentioned in the promotional material,

---

[6] *Calamity Jane: The Woman and the Legend,* Page 192
[7] *Calamity Jane: The Woman and the Legend,* Page 192.

possibly because she joined the show after it had begun.

A week after she had joined the expo, Jane broke the agreement that she made with Brake to avoid alcohol. Mattie Dorsett, as the local paper called her, was arrested and taken to a Buffalo jail after being discovered drunk outside the gates of the expo. It was just the beginning of her troubles in New York, where she was not finding the same level of tolerance for her drunken ways as she did in the West. At one point, she reportedly fell in love with Frederick Darlington and rumors circulated that they might get married.

Overall, Jane was miserable on the East Coast, but at first she insisted she did not have the money to return home. By September, though, she had begun her journey back west with the assistance of Bill Cody, who gave her money for the train, plus a little extra. Of course, the extra funds were used for alcohol. It took Jane several months before she eventually returned to familiar territory, spending some time in Pierre and then, nine months after she had departed, Montana. The Billings newspaper reported that on her first night back, she was arrested for drunken and disorderly conduct. From there it was to Livingstone, which was not too happy to see her either, and then on to communities near Yellowstone Park that were less likely to care too much about her intoxication.

Inevitably, Jane's health continued to decline as she moved from town to town. Due to her fame, and the fact that everyone around her knew she was an alcoholic, there were many people who tried to help her by taking donations. And despite how the experience in Buffalo ended, Josephine Brake was prodding the government to get Jane an Army pension, still unaware that Jane had invented the story about being an army scout. On the other hand, there were people who felt that Jane had already had more than her fair share of assistance, considering she had done little of significance to warrant her fame. To many, the famous Calamity Jane was a relic of the past and a burden to society.

On November 21, 1902, Jane was arrested in Montana for allegedly attacking a store clerk with a hatchet, and the local papers noted that her behavior had become increasingly erratic. Drunken binges and arrests marked her final weeks of life as she left Montana for the last time in December and returned to the Black Hills. In Bella Fourche, Jane cooked and did laundry for the ladies of the evening at Madam Dora DuFran, one of the West's most well-known and successful madams. She was able to stay sober for about six weeks, but she resumed her drinking ways after that. Those that saw her in her final months said she looked like she was in her 70s, not her 50s.

Dora DuFran

In July 1903, Jane took a train headed for Terry Country, South Dakota and became so ill on the train that the conductor had to help her off the train and get her a room at the Calloway Hotel. The years of alcohol abuse had finally caught up with her. Calamity Jane died in the hotel on August 1, 1903 at the age of 51.

Given her legend and legacy, it was fitting that Calamity Jane was ultimately buried alongside Wild Bill, though the reasons for it have long been debated. It was said that Calamity Jane visited Wild Bill Hickok's grave often, and that he had been reinterred and moved at her request. Wild Bill was initially laid to rest in Ingleside Cemetery in Deadwood, but after the cemetery filled up, Wild Bill was moved to Mount Moriah Cemetery. Part of the legend of Calamity Jane is that she supposedly asked to be buried next to Hickok as her dying request, while others say that because Wild Bill had no use for her in life, she was buried next to him for all eternity as a joke. However, the most likely explanation is that town officials in Deadwood decided to bury Calamity Jane next to Wild Bill Hickok to boost tourism. Wild Bill's wife, Agnes, who never saw Hickok again after he left Cincinnati to join the gold rush to the Black Hills, was buried next to her first husband instead of Hickok when she died in 1907.

Chapter 6: The Legend of Calamity Jane

Many of the Wild West icons are based at least in part on fiction, but perhaps none as much as Calamity Jane. An assessment of her life shows that she did little more than be present at a mythical time in American history, as the country expanded to the western frontier. The fascination with Calamity Jane was actually based on the public's fascination with the West and admiration for accomplishments she never truly achieved. Jane understood this in her later years, but few could blame her for cashing in and profiting from her fame.

Simply assessing her life as a woman of the late 19th century, Martha Canary was arguably a victim of unfortunate circumstances. Orphaned at a young age with no adult role model, she did what she could do to survive. Not unlike young men and women of the generations that followed her, she turned to alcohol, perhaps to ease pain or maybe as a way to fit in. Whatever the reason, alcoholism was a demon that she could never escape and ultimately cost Martha her life.

As was the case during her life, popular culture has largely been uninterested in the truth about the woman behind Calamity Jane. The most enduring myth is the notion that she had a romance with Wild Bill Hickok. The 1936 movie "The Plainsmen", starring Gary Cooper as Hickok and Jean Arthur as Calamity Jane, and a 1984 television movie on CBS called "Calamity Jane", both fed into the idea. The 1995 movie "Wild Bill", which stars Jeff Bridges as Hickok and Ellen Barkin as Calamity Jane," portray their relationship as an off-again, on-again romance. Their alleged romance was also made into a musical in 1953, with Doris Day playing Calamity Jane in the film of the same name. The musical capitalized on the popularity of "Annie Get Your Gun," the successful movie about the sharpshooting Western icon Annie Oakley, but Annie was the polar opposite of Martha Canary in behavior and lifestyle. It seems that a romance between Wild Bill and Calamity Jane makes for a better story than the truth.

Calamity Jane has been portrayed on television several times too. In 1963, Carol Burnett took on the role of Calamity Jane in the television adaption of the "Calamity Jane" film starring Doris Day. In 1984, Jane Alexander was nominated for an Emmy for her take on Calamity Jane in the movie "Calamity Jane", which dramatized a marriage between Jane and Hickok and mentions a child they had together but was given up for adoption. The daughter, played by 7 year-old Melissa Gilbert, is Jean McCormick, the woman who fraudulently claimed that Martha and Hickok were her parents decades earlier. In 1997, a French producer created the television cartoon "The Legend of Calamity Jane" for the WB network. Perhaps the most accurate portrayal of Calamity Jane came from Robin Weigert, who played Jane true to her hard-drinking, foul-mouthed ways in the acclaimed HBO series "Deadwood" in 2005. The performance earned Weigert an Emmy nomination.

Since Martha Canary's life had few accomplishments worthy of merit, perhaps the real question to ask is why pop culture remains so interested in her. Her name and likeness are still used to sell any number of things, ranging from golf clubs to handbags to women's lingerie. Over 100 years after her death, Calamity Jane remains a recurring character in books and on film, and she is still one of the most famous residents of Deadwood. The answer to her enduring popularity seems to lie in the ongoing fascination with the West and with individualism. Martha's rise to fame and the fact that she claimed the official title of "Calamity Jane," even though there were other women that lived in her era with that nickname, is part of why Americans continue to revere the romanticized notion of the frontier and the Wild West. For Americans, the West represents freedom and independence, and while Martha Canary will always be known more for things she didn't actually do, nobody can deny that Calamity Jane was independent and adventurous.

The Life and Adventures of Calamity Jane

In 1896, Calamity Jane had published a short autobiographical statement about her life in conjunction with her making appearances in a circus that year. Since she was illiterate, it's unclear who exactly wrote it out, but it got her date of birth wrong, the spelling of the name Missouri wrong, and likely the spelling of her last name wrong. But given that she was known to embellish and even falsify details of her life, it's presumable that she dictated the statement to whoever wrote it down.

The account is reproduced below:

My maiden name was Marthy Cannary. I was born in Princeton, Missourri, May 1st, 1852. Father and mother were natives of Ohio. I had two brothers and three sisters, I being the oldest of the children. As a child I always had a fondness for adventure and out-door exercise and especial fondness for horses which I began to ride at an early age and continued to do so until I became an expert rider being able to ride the most vicious and stubborn of horses, in fact the greater portion of my life in early times was spent in this manner.

In 1865 we emigrated from our homes in Missourri by the overland route to Virginia City, Montana, taking five months to make the journey. While on the way the greater portion of my time was spent in hunting along with the men and hunters of the party, in fact I was at all times with the men when there was excitement and adventures to be had. By the time we reached Virginia City I was considered a remarkable good shot and a fearless rider for a girl of my age. I remember many occurrences on the journey from Missourri to Montana. Many times in crossing the mountains the conditions of the trail were so bad that we frequently had to lower the wagons over ledges by hand with ropes for they were so rough and rugged that horses were of no use. We also had many exciting times fording streams for many of the streams in our way were noted for quicksands and boggy places, where, unless we were very careful, we would have lost horses and all. Then we had many dangers to encounter in the way of streams swelling on account of heavy rains. On occasions of that kind the men would usually select the best places to cross the streams, myself on more than one occasion have mounted my pony and swam across the stream several times merely to amuse myself and have had many narow escapes from having both myself and pony washed away to certain death, but as the pioneers of those days had plenty of courage we overcame all obstacles and reached Virginia City in safety.

Mother died at Black Foot, Montana, 1866, where we buried her. I left Montana in Spring of 1866, for Utah, arriving at Salt Lake city during the summer. Remained in Utah until 1867, where my father died, then went to Fort Bridger, Wyoming Territory, where we arrived May 1, 1868, then went to Piedmont, Wyoming, with U.P. Railway. Joined General Custer as a scout at Fort Russell, Wyoming, in 1870, and started for Arizona for the Indian Campaign. Up to this time I had always worn the costume of my sex. When I joined Custer I donned the uniform of a soldier. It was a bit awkward at first but I soon got to be perfectly at home in men's clothes.

Was in Arizona up to the winter of 1871 and during that time I had a great many adventures with the Indians, for as a scout I had a great many dangerous missions to perform and while I was in many close places always succeeded in getting away safely for by this time I was considered the most reckless and daring rider and one of the best shots in the western country.

After that campaign I returned to Fort Sanders, Wyoming, remained there until spring of 1872, when we were ordered out to the Muscle Shell or Nursey Pursey Indian outbreak. In that war Generals Custer, Miles, Terry and Crook were all engaged. This campaign lasted until fall of 1873.

It was during this campaign that I was christened Calamity Jane. It was on Goose Creek, Wyoming, where the town of Sheridan is now located. Capt. Egan was in command of the Post. We were ordered out to quell an uprising of the Indians, and were out for several days, had numerous skirmishes during which six of the soldiers were killed and several severely wounded. When on returning to the Post we were ambushed about a mile and a half from our destination. When fired upon Capt. Egan was shot. I was riding in advance and on hearing the firing turned in my saddle and saw the Captain reeling in his saddle as though about to fall. I turned my horse and galloped back with all haste to his side and got there in time to catch him as he was falling. I lifted him onto my horse in front of me and succeeded in getting him safely to the Fort. Capt. Egan on recovering, laughingly said: "I name you Calamity Jane, the heroine of the plains." I have borne that name up to the present time. We were afterwards ordered to Fort Custer, where Custer city now stands, where we arrived in the spring of 1874; remained around Fort Custer all summer and were ordered to Fort Russell in fall of 1874, where we remained until spring of 1875; was then ordered to the Black Hills to protect miners, as that country was controlled by the Sioux Indians and the government had to send the soldiers to protect the lives of the miners and settlers in that section. Remained there until fall of 1875 and wintered at Fort Laramie. In spring of 1876, we were ordered north with General Crook to join Gen'ls Miles, Terry and Custer at Big Horn river. During this march I swam the Platte river at Fort Fetterman as I was the bearer of important dispatches. I had a ninety mile ride to make, being wet and cold, I contracted a severe illness and was sent back in Gen. Crook's ambulance to Fort Fetterman where I laid in the hospital for fourteen days. When able to ride I started for Fort Laramie where I met Wm. Hickock, better known as Wild Bill, and we started for Deadwood, where we arrived about June.

During the month of June I acted as a pony express rider carrying the U.S. mail between Deadwood and Custer, a distance of fifty miles, over one of the roughest trails in the Black Hills country. As many of the riders before me had been held up and robbed of their packages, mail and money that they carried, for that was the only means of getting mail and money between these points. It was considered the most dangerous route in the Hills, but as my reputation as a rider and quick shot was well known, I was molested very little, for the toll gatherers looked on me as being a good fellow, and they knew that I never missed my mark. I made the round trip every two days which was considered pretty good riding in that country. Remained around Deadwood all that summer visiting all the camps within an area of one hundred miles. My friend, Wild Bill, remained in Deadwood during the summer with the exception of occasional visits to the camps. On the 2nd of August, while setting at a gambling table in the Bell Union saloon, in Deadwood, he was shot in the back of the head by the notorious Jack McCall, a desperado. I was in Deadwood at the time and on hearing of the killing made my way at once to the scene of the shooting and found that my friend had been killed by McCall. I at once started to look for the assassian and found him at Shurdy's butcher shop and grabbed a meat cleaver and made him throw up his hands; through the excitement on hearing of Bill's death, having left my weapons on the post of my bed. He was then taken to a log cabin and locked up, well secured as every one thought, but he got away and was afterwards caught at Fagan's ranch on Horse Creek, on the old Cheyenne road and was then taken to Yankton, Dak., where he was tried, sentenced and hung.

I remained around Deadwood locating claims, going from camp to camp until the spring of 1877, where one morning, I saddled my horse and rode towards Crook city. I had gone about twelve miles from Deadwood, at the mouth of Whitewood creek, when I met the overland mail running from Cheyenne to Deadwood. The horses on a run, about two hundred yards from the station; upon looking closely I saw they were pursued by Indians. The horses ran to the barn as was their custom. As the horses stopped I rode along side of the coach and found the driver John Slaughter, lying face downwards in the boot of the stage, he having been shot by the Indians. When the stage got to the station the Indians hid in the bushes. I immediately removed all baggage from the coach except the mail. I then took the driver's seat and with all haste drove to Deadwood, carrying the six passengers and the dead driver.

I left Deadwood in the fall of 1877, and went to Bear Butte Creek with the 7th Cavalry. During the fall and winter we built Fort Meade and the town of Sturgis. In 1878 I left the command and went to Rapid city and put in the year prospecting.

In 1879 I went to Fort Pierre and drove trains from Rapid city to Fort Pierre for Frank Wite then drove teams from Fort Pierce to Sturgis for Fred. Evans. This teaming was done with oxen as they were better fitted for the work than horses, owing to the rough nature of the country.

In 1881 I went to Wyoming and returned in 1882 to Miles city and took up a ranch on the Yellow Stone, raising stock and cattle, also kept a way side inn, where the weary traveler could be accommodated with food, drink, or trouble if he looked for it. Left the ranch in 1883, went to California, going through the States and territories, reached Ogden the latter part of 1883, and San Francisco in 1884. Left San Francisco in the summer of 1884 for Texas, stopping at Fort Yuma, Arizona, the hottest spot in the United States. Stopping at all points of interest until I reached El Paso in the fall. While in El Paso, I met Mr. Clinton Burk, a native of Texas, who I married in August 1885. As I thought I had travelled through life long enough alone and thought it was about time to take a partner for the rest of my days. We remained in Texas leading a quiet home life until 1889. On October 28th, 1887, I became the mother of a girl baby, the very image of its father, at least that is what he said, but who has the temper of its mother.

When we left Texas we went to Boulder, Colo., where we kept a hotel until 1893, after which we travelled through Wyoming, Montana, Idaho, Washington, Oregon, then back to Montana, then to Dakota, arriving in Deadwood October 9th, 1895, after an absence of seventeen years.

My arrival in Deadwood after an absence of so many years created quite an excitement among my many friends of the past, to such an extent that a vast number of the citizens who had come to Deadwood during my absence who had heard so much of Calamity Jane and her many adventures in former years were anxious to see me. Among the many whom I met were several gentlemen from eastern cities who advised me to allow myself to be placed before the public in such a manner as to give the people of the eastern cities an opportunity of seeing the Woman Scout who was made so famous through her daring career in the West and Black Hill countries.

An agent of Kohl & Middleton, the celebrated Museum men came to Deadwood, through the solicitation of the gentleman who I had met there and arrangements were made to place me before the public in this manner. My first engagement began at the Palace Museum, Minneapolis, January 20th, 1896, under Kohl and Middleton's management.

Hoping that this little history of my life may interest all readers, I remain as in the older days,

Yours,

Mrs. M. BURK

BETTER KNOWN AS CALAMITY JANE

Bibliography

Deadwood Magazine. "Calamity Jane Was Part of the Overhead." 2001. Accessed November 14, 2012. http://www.deadwoodmagazine.com/archivedsite/Archives/Girls_Calamity.htm.

McLaird, James D. *Calamity Jane: The Woman and the Legend.* Norman, OK: University of Oklahoma Press. 2005.

McLaird, James. *Wild Bill Hickok and Calamity Jane: Deadwood Legends.* [Kindle version]. Retrieved from Amazon.com. 2008.

Slatta, Richard W. *The Mythical West: An Encyclopedia of Legend, Lore, and Popular Culture.* Santa Barbara, CA: ABC-CLIO. 2001.

Riley, Glenda and Richard W. Etulain. *Wild Women of the West.* Golden, CO: Fulcrum Publishing. 2003.

Made in the USA
Middletown, DE
19 December 2016